Fun with English

Good Words

WILLIAM EDMONDS

KING*f*ISHER

The author wishes to express his particular gratitude to Robert Wheeler, the designer of all the books in this series. There has been an especially close collaboration at every stage and the author has found this an immense stimulus and encouragement. The author would also like to thank Terry McKenna for his superbly amusing illustrations, invaluable ingredients of the series.

KINGFISHER
Kingfisher Publications Plc
New Penderel House, 283–288 High Holborn,
London WC1V 7HZ

The material in this edition was previously published by Kingfisher Publications Plc in the *Wordmaster* series (1993) and in the *Guide to Good English* series (1989)

This edition published by Kingfisher Publications Plc 1999
10 9 8 7 6 5 4 3 2 1
1TR/0399/EDK/(ATL)/140EDI

This edition copyright © Kingfisher Publications Plc 1995
Text copyright © William Edmonds 1989
Illustrations copyright © Kingfisher Publications Plc
1989, 1993

A CIP catalogue record for this book is available from the British Library

ISBN 0 7534 0369 2

Printed in Spain

The Treasures

Words

Words are Wonderful

We speak with words
    and we listen to words.

We write words
    and we read words.

And we think with words.

We humans are so lucky. We are the only creatures on earth to have such wonderful treasures:

✳ Words as tools
Words are tools which we use to communicate with each other. We use them to talk, discuss, argue, agree, describe, plan, organize, remember, sing, imagine and do all manner of things to help us live and thrive.

✳ Words as jewels
When we take care to choose just the right words they become like glittering jewels. They are a great pleasure to listen to and read. Everybody wants to know what they are about.

This A to Z guide is like a small treasure chest. Open it and you will find 40 different kinds of word, including all the important 'parts of speech' (marked by a *).

BE WARNED! Good words are impossible to resist.

☐ Abbreviations

An abbreviation is a short way of writing a word or group of words. Sometimes it is just a part of a full word. Sometimes it is made up of initial letters.

* Some kinds of abbreviations are used by everybody:

Thomas

Titles:	Names	Countries
Mr for mister	*Tom* for Thomas	*U.K. (G.B.)*
Mrs for missus	*Ben* for Benjamin	*U.S.A.*
Col. for colonel	*Pat* for Patricia	*U.S.S.R.*

Several words, like *phone, photo, maths, TV* are better known as abbreviations than in their full form.

A few English abbreviations come from other languages:
RSVP for 'répondez s'il vous plaît' – French for *please reply.*
NB for 'nota bene'   Latin for *note well.*
AD for Anno Domini – Latin for *in the year of the Lord.*

Patricia

* Other kinds of abbreviations are ones that we make for ourselves or use just with people that we know. They can be a kind of slang like *brill* for brilliant or *telly* for television.

> Have you any good abbreviations for the names of your friends?

☐ Acronyms

An acronym is a kind of abbreviation. It is a word formed from the initial or first letters of a group of other words.

Benjamin

*LASER (***L**ight **A**mplification by **S**timulated **E**mission of **R**adiation)
RADAR (**RA**dio **D**etection **A**nd **R**anging)
SCUBA (**S**elf-**C**ontained **U**nderwater **B**reathing **A**pparatus)

Beautiful,
black cats

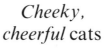

Smelly,
smoking cats

Cheeky,
cheerful cats

Angry,
awkward cats

☐ Adjectives*

Adjectives are words that tell us what something or somebody is like.

Did you know, for instance, that there were so many different kinds of cat?

Zoo cats

These words about cats are all being used as adjectives, although sometimes they can be used as other parts of speech. *Zoo* and *jelly*, for instance, are better known as **nouns**, but occasionally, as here, we can use nouns as adjectives. Also we can make certain verbs into adjectives: cats that lie down and watch out can become *lying* and *watchful* cats.

How about making an A to Z of adjectives for something else that you like: kinds of people, days, houses, ideas or whatever?

Watchful,
wily cats

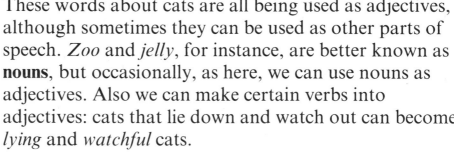

Vicious,
vigorous cats

Ugly,
undesirable
cats

Young,
yellow cats

Excellent
cats

Tame,
tabby cats

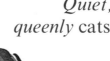

Quiet,
queenly cats

Daft, destructive cats

Fat, fishy cats

Enormous cats

Great, greedy cats

Adjectives can help to put sparkle into writing. Choose them carefully, to make them vary and to make sure that they say exactly what you mean. Certain adjectives, such as *nice, great, lovely* or *cute* can be used too often, and so make writing rather dull and vague.

Happy cats

Great adjectives

splendid
outstanding
famous
brilliant
wonderful
important

GREAT

enormous
huge
gigantic
incredible
fantastic
terrific
super

Intelligent, interesting cats

Jolly, jelly cats

Rowdy, rascally cats

Lazy, lying cats

Kind, knowledgeable cats

Obstinate, odd cats

Mischievous, miserly cats

Nosy, noisy cats

Practical, pleasing cats

☐ Adverbs*

An adverb is a word which tells you *how* something is done, whether, for instance, it is done *quickly, efficiently, neatly, badly* or *well*. It adds to a verb.

There are many ways of walking: *fast, slowly, backwards, stupidly, stiffly, purposefully, lightly, thoughtfully, carelessly* or *dangerously*.

"And there are many ways of talking,"
  she said *very loudly*.
"No need to shout,"
  he answered *coolly*.
"I thought you were deaf,"
  she added *angrily*.
"No, I can hear you *perfectly well*,"
  he said *politely*.
"Well, I was going to say that
  we need to use adverbs to
  be clear about the different ways
  of talking or shouting,"
  she finished *more calmly*.

Select (*jokingfully*, if you like) some adverbs for different ways of eating, writing, singing or driving.

Adverbs can often be made out of adjectives: the cats played *awkwardly, cheekily,* and so on.
They can answer the questions When? Where? How? How often? and so on.
Adverbs may also add to adjectives or other adverbs:

very beautiful,
amazingly handsome
or *unspeakably, revoltingly* ugly.

amazingly
handsome

☐ Antonyms

An antonym is a word which is opposite in meaning to another word.

> long   – short
> clever – stupid
> enemy   – friend
> safe   – dangerous

> difficult – easy
> shallow – deep
> fast   – slow
> huge   – tiny

Sometimes an antonym can be made by adding a **prefix** such as *un-* or *dis-*

kind – unkind   *like   – dislike*
do   – undo   *appear – disappear*

Antonyms can help us to think clearly about the meanings of words and, just occasionally, they can be a good test of the imagination.

☐ Articles*

As well as being things or pieces of writing, articles are particular kinds of words, ones that introduce other words.

There is the **definite article:** *the*.
The definite article is so called because when we use it we are definite about which one we mean – the article in the newspaper has to be one particular article.

And there is the **indefinite article:** *a* or *an*.
The indefinite article is so called because we are not definite about what is being referred to – an article in a newspaper could mean any old article from anywhere.

It is important to take care in choosing which indefinite article to use – *a* or *an*.

a comes before words beginning with consonants.
an goes before words beginning with vowels (*a e i o u*).

A white Rabbit

An amazing Rabbit

　　　an amazing rabbit – *a* white rabbit

9

☐ Beautiful words

> *crocodile, snooker, exquisite, anaconda, O, marmalade.*
> *marigold, indigo, glorious, cinnamon, extravaganza,*

Beautiful words are really a matter of personal taste.

> Can you name and frame some which *you* think are really beautiful?

☐ Borrowed Words

Many English words are borrowed from other languages. Here are a few to show how world-wide the borrowing has been:

automatic (Greek) *judo* (Japanese) *safari* (Swahili)
banana (West African) *khaki* (Urdu) *tea* (Chinese)
curry (Tamil) *limerick* (Irish) *ukelele* (Hawaiian)
pyjamas (Hindu) *mattress* (Arabic) *vodka* (Russian)
gingham (Malay) *piano* (Italian) *yacht* (Dutch)
hamburger (German) *robot* (Czech) *zebra* (Bantu)

☐ Brief words

We say that we have had a brief word with someone when we mean we have had a short conversation. That's all.

> There are over 30 two-letter words in the English language. How many can you write?

Hi! bye! OK ALL Right

☐ Common confusions

Here are a few pairs of almost similar words which often cause confusion:

affect *effect*	In the common use of these words *affect* is a verb (Smoking may *affect* your health) and *effect* is a noun (Smoking can have dangerous *effects* on your health).
complement *compliment*	*Complement* means to fill out to make whole; *compliment* means to praise.
disinterested *uninterested*	*Disinterested* means being impartial, unbiased. *Uninterested* suggests a lack of all interest.
emigrate *immigrate*	*Emigrate* means to move to another country; *immigrate* means to come from another country.
principal *principle*	*Principal* can be a noun meaning chief (She is *principal* of a college) or an adjective (My *principal* reason is . . .). *Principle* is only a noun and means a fundamental belief (I refuse on *principle*).
stationery *stationary*	*Stationery* refers to writing materials whereas *stationary* means staying still.

The best way of checking words which are easily confused is to use a good dictionary.

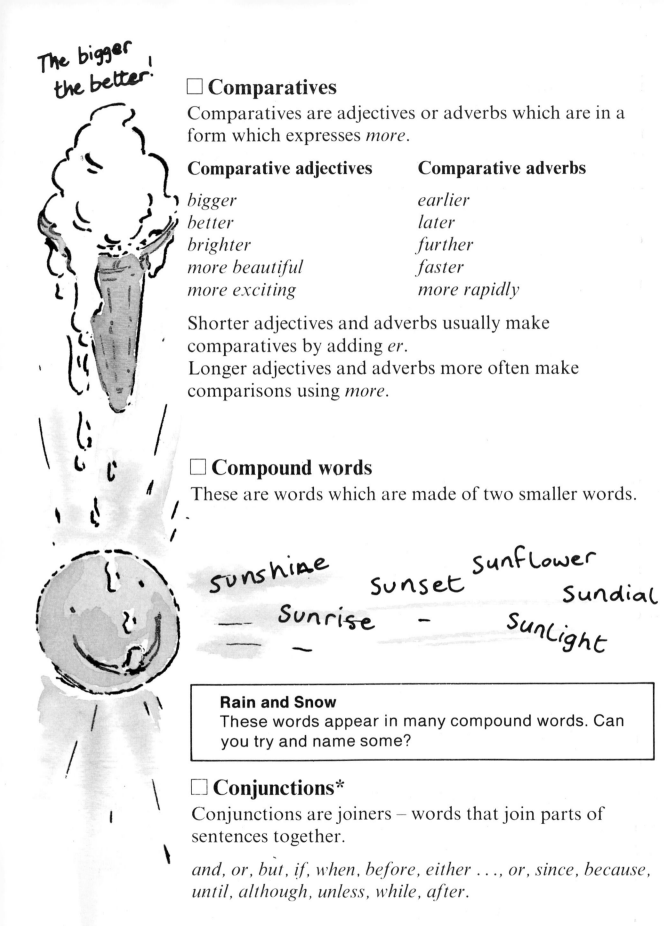

The bigger the better!

☐ Comparatives

Comparatives are adjectives or adverbs which are in a form which expresses _more_.

Comparative adjectives	Comparative adverbs
bigger	_earlier_
better	_later_
brighter	_further_
more beautiful	_faster_
more exciting	_more rapidly_

Shorter adjectives and adverbs usually make comparatives by adding _er_.
Longer adjectives and adverbs more often make comparisons using _more_.

☐ Compound words

These are words which are made of two smaller words.

sunshine   _sunset_   _sunflower_
sunrise   –   _sundial_
sunlight

> **Rain and Snow**
> These words appear in many compound words. Can you try and name some?

☐ Conjunctions*

Conjunctions are joiners – words that join parts of sentences together.

and, or, but, if, when, before, either . . ., or, since, because, until, although, unless, while, after.

Rock 'n Roll

☐ Contractions

Contractions are words which are combined and then shortened by taking out one or more letters. The place of the missing letters is usually filled with an apostrophe (').

n't (not)	*'d* (had, would)
can't (cannot), *couldn't* (could not), *don't, doesn't, didn't, hasn't. wouldn't, couldn't, won't,* (will not).	*he'd* (he would or he had), *we'd, I'd, you'd, they'd.*

'll (will)	*'ve* (have)	*'re* (are)
he'll (he will), *I'll* and so on.	*I've* (I have), *we've* (we have)	*We're* (we are).

's (is, has)
she's (she is, or she has) and *it's* (it is) – not to be confused with *its* with no apostrophe, meaning belonging to it.

It is often the case that we use contractions more when we talk than when we write. If you are not sure which form to use, or want to be formal and polite, it is probably best to use the full words.

☐ Diminutives

Diminutives are words that indicate smaller versions of things or creatures.

booklet, piglet, duckling, kitchenette, hillock, miniskirt.

They are usually made by adding **suffixes** (*-let, -ling, -et, -ette, -kin, -ock*) or the **prefix** *mini.*

The young of animals give rise to a lot of special names:

Tadpoles

Owlets

fawns

foals

Calves

chicks   Puppies   Spry   cygnets   Cubs   Lambs

Kittens   bunnies   elvers   leverets

☐ Euphemisms

Euphemisms are words which make some things seem a little more pleasant or more easy to accept than if a more direct word was used.

Passing away is a euphemism sometimes used for dying. *Toilet* (originally meaning 'getting dressed and made up') or *lavatory* (originally meaning 'a washing place or vessel') are words that have many other euphemisms: *convenience, WC (water closet), Gentlemen, Gents, Ladies, cloakroom, bathroom, restroom* and so on.

> ### *Not very nice*
> This can be a euphemism for all kinds of words and expressions. Perhaps you can suggest ways of being blunt and direct about something you don't approve of.

☐ Exclamations

These are words which exclaim, so as to show warning, surprise, urgency, horror, disappointment and so on.

☐ Expletives

These are kinds of **exclamations** which are used for expressing really strong feelings of disgust, frustration, sudden pain or anger.

Ouch!

Eek!

Bother!

Damnation

☐ Exploding words

EXPLOSION

BAAAAANG!

CRRRAAAASSSSSSH!

Now explode these words: *ATTISHOO!* *SPLASH!*

☐ Happy Words

roses puppies jolly birthday merriment

sunshine warmth party

dancing skipping twinkling bubbles candles

cherries apples strawberries ringing and singing family friends

brilliance

pleasure leisure excitement ecstasy excellence

ice cream swimming pool sympathy soothing songs

presents splendour wonder magnificence

Christmas

tingle sprinkle sparkle

Happiness is . . . . Can you describe a truly happy moment of your own?

☐ Homonyms

A homonym (taken from two Greek words: *homo* – meaning same – and *nym* – meaning name) is a word which has one spelling but more than one meaning. Here are examples:

coach, match, race, ram, saw, stamp, tie, watch.

Homonyms are often found in riddles.

1 Why are rivers handy places for collecting money?

2 When is a guilty person like a firework?

3 Why are waiters good at sums?

Watch
Watch!

> **3** Because they know their *tables.*
> **2** When they can both be *let off.*
> **1** Because they have *banks* on either side.

☐ Homophones

A homophone (taken from the Greek words meaning *same* and *sound*) is a word which has the same sound as another word but has a different spelling.

fair/fare, meet/meat, there/their, see/sea.

These kinds of words can easily cause confusion with spelling. They can also lead to clever double meanings and funny jokes.

> Do you know about the three sons who took over a cattle ranch from their father? They called it Focus because it is where *the sun's rays meet/the sons raise meat.*

do you have trouble with the hare on your hair?

Jokes and riddles using homophones are best when they are told and not just read. This kind of word play is known as making a pun. Puns often come to *sighs/size*!

17

☐ Imperatives

Imperatives are words which are used for giving orders. They are verbs used in a basic form (infinitive without the 'to').

Be quiet!

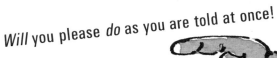
Will you please *do* as you are told at once!

Come here!

Stop that horrible noise!

Listen to me!

Don't do that any more!

Children often have to put up with hearing imperatives.

> What are some of the favourite imperatives used by your parents or teachers?

☐ Interrogatives*

These are words which introduce questions.

Why is there so much salt in the sea?
Where is the Sargasso Sea?
How did the world begin?
Who invented toothpaste?
When will pigs learn to fly?

> *Why* oh *why*? Why not ask a few questions yourself about pigs, planets, people or whatever?

☐ Journalese

Journalese refers to the kinds of words that journalists like to use in newspapers.
They like their writing to be 'punchy', using simple words in a way which is dramatic and eye-catching.

Children hit by Teachers' strike

SHOPKEEPER SLAMS COUNCIL

THIEVES GEM SNATCH

☐ Kennings

Kennings are unusual descriptions which are used in place of names. They are often like riddles.

goggle box (T.V.) Adam's ale (water)
ship of the desert (camel)

Goggle box

Four stiff standers
Four dilly danders
Two lookers
Two crookers
And a wig wag

4 legs,
4 teats,
2 eyes,
2 horns
and a tail

magic power

☐ Nouns*

Nouns are naming words. We use them to label anything that can be seen, heard or thought.
You name it – it's a noun.

Nouns have a kind of magic power. When we speak or write a noun we can conjure up a picture of it in our mind. Nouns let us talk, write or think about anything we like without having to have it around.

* We can whet our appetite by looking at all the nouns on a menu.

Menu
1
Steak
Sausages
bacon

Hamburger
CHIPS
lemonade

Coke
Ice cream
chocolate
Vanilla
Strawberry

* We can make lists of nouns to be bought from the shops.

Sugar
eggs
Jam
honey
bread
milk
Coffee
peanut butter

20

* We can check time
   nouns on
   a calendar.

* We can collect nouns from all around us: in the
   kitchen, in the bedroom, in the cupboard, under the
   floorboards, outside in the garden, in the street, in
   the countryside, at sea, in the sky, in space or just in
   the head.

The Kitchen
*cooker, fridge, knife, fork, bowl, plate, cloth, sink, butter,
eggs, floor, mess . . .*

Collect some nouns for your bedroom or other places
that you like,

* We can play games with nouns.

   I spy with my little eye . . .

* We can use nouns to make stories.

Once upon a time there was a beautiful ....
(**common noun**).
She was called .... (**proper noun**). She lived in
a .... (**c.n.**) near a .... (**c.n.**).

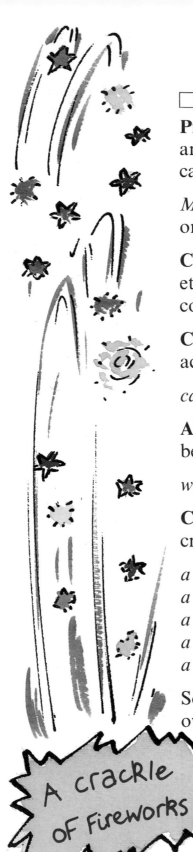

☐ Noun groups*

Proper nouns: those which name particular people, animals, places and times. They always begin with capital letters.

Mary Jones and *Spot* (the dog) at *Birmingham* on *Friday*.

Common nouns: those which name the kind of person, etc. rather than naming a particular one. They can be concrete nouns, abstract nouns or collective nouns.

Concrete nouns are the names of anything that can actually be seen or touched.

cabbages, kings, computers, cogs, helicopters, hedgehogs.

Abstract nouns are the names of anything that can only be thought about and not seen or touched.

wind, noise, happiness, poverty, honesty, idea.

Collective nouns are used to name a collection of creatures or things.

a herd of cows   *a flock of sheep*
a gaggle of geese   *a pride of lions*
a pack of wolves   *a pack of cards*
a clump of trees   *a swarm of bees*
a company of actors   *a gang of thieves*

Sometimes it is fun to make up collective nouns of one's own, how about:

A crackle of fireworks

A talkshop of teachers

Spin of spiders

What might be good collective nouns for helicopters, hedgehogs, or ghosts?

☐ Personal Words

A few words are taken from the names of people who first invented or used something.

Hooligan
This is taken from the name, Houlihan, the head of an Irish family who lived in London and were well known for their noisy and unruly behaviour.

Wellington boots
These were named after the Duke of Wellington, a British general, who wore knee-high riding boots specially made for him.

Lord *Sandwich*, Giuseppi *Garibaldi*, Charles *Mackintosh*, Daniel *Fahrenheit*, Ladilao *Biro* and Lord *Cardigan* also had their names given to things which we all know about today, even if we have forgotten about the people.

How about inventing something to be named after your own name?

☐ Prefixes

A prefix is that part of a word which is sometimes added (fixed) at the beginning.

pre- (meaning *before*) is the prefix of prefix, prehistoric, and predict.

un- (not or reverse) as in unhappy, untidy, undo, unwind.

mis- (wrong) as in mistake, mispell, misapply, misdeed.

a-, fore-, co- (with), *circum-* (around), *semi-* (half), *re-* (again), *super-* (above), *trans-* (across), *ob-* (against), *poly-* (many), *tele-* (from afar), and *vice-* (in place of) are among the common prefixes. Many of them come from Latin and Greek words.

Autosuggestion (self-suggestion)
How many *auto-* words can you yourself suggest?

Co –
star
operate
incidental
habit
here
education

Where is it?

What's all this about you and me?

☐ Prepositions*

A preposition is a word which tells where something is in relation to something else.

Where is the missing pencil?
Is it *in* the living room, *on* the floor, *by* the television, *over* there, *under* the newspaper, *with* the other pencils, *in front of* you, *behind* you, *up on* the shelf, *out of* reach, *down* there, *through* the hall or is it *right beside* you?

Directions
See how many different prepositions you can use to describe the way *to* your nearest post office.

☐ Pronouns*

Pronouns are words used in place of nouns. There are really five kinds of pronouns.

Personal pronouns
I, you, he, she, it, we, they, me, him, her, us, them.

Relative pronouns
who, whose, whom, which, that.

Possessive pronouns
mine, yours, his, hers, its, ours, theirs.

Interrogative pronouns
What? Who? Which? Whom? Whose?

Demonstrative pronouns
this, these, that, those.

24

☐ Regional Words

These refer to English words that particular countries or regions keep as their own. We can see this, for instance, in some of the differences between British and North American words, or between Australian and British words.

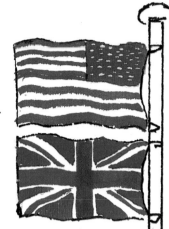

American	British
apartment	flat
closet	cupboard
cookies	biscuits
elevator	lift
fall	autumn
faucet	tap
gas(olene)	petrol
sidewalk	pavement

Australian	British
creek	stream
outback	countryside
paddock	(any) field
squatter	farmer
whinge	complain

These are good examples of how words can change from place to place and from time to time. They demonstrate the richness of the English language.

☐ Slang

Slang is the name given to words which we like to use when talking with people we know. They are not usually regarded as acceptable for serious conversation or for writing. Common slang words change with fashion.

Certain words such as idiot, money, clever and good have a lot of substitute slang words.

Idiot   *wally, burk, goon, twit, noodle.*

Money   *dough, smackers, greens, readies.*

Clever   *brainy, egghead.*

Good   *magic, smashing, ace, brilliant, groovy.*

What is the latest slang that you have heard for these words?

Enjoy Enjoyable Endings!

☐ Suffixes

A suffix is that part of a word which is sometimes added (fixed) at the end – a word ending. If you understand about suffixes you can use them to build up thousands of words.

With *-able, -al, -age,* and *-an* we can change the words enjoy, music, marry, suburb into *enjoyable, musical, marriage, suburban.*

-ary, -ate, -ess (for female forms) as in actress and tigress), *-ful, -fy, -ish, -ism, -ity, -less, -ment* and *-ness* are among the many common suffixes.

> Effortless Cleverness
> Try making adjectives turn into abstract nouns
> by adding *-ness, goodness* . . .
> And try making nouns turn into adjectives
> by adding *-less, mindless* . . .

☐ Superlatives

Superlatives are adjectives or adverbs which are in a form which expresses *most*.

Superlative adjectives
biggest
best
worst
most difficult

Superlative adverbs
latest
soonest
most disgustingly
most fortunately

only the best

☐ Syllables

A syllable is a section or part of a word which can be said by itself.

Ambulance has three syllables: *am-bu-lance*
Good has only one syllable: *good*
Examination has five: *ex-am-in-a-tion*.

☐ Synonyms

A synonym is a word which has the same meaning as another one.

quick – fast, annually – yearly, vacant – empty

A Thesaurus is a book which provides an alphabetical list of words with their synonyms. Using synonyms is a way of avoiding tedious repetition of one word and therefore of helping to make your writing more interesting.

Quick   Fast

☐ Tongue Twisters

These are words deliberately placed together to make them difficult to speak out aloud without twisting the tongue in knots.

I miss my Swiss, my Swiss miss misses me.
I miss the bliss that Swiss kiss gives to me.

A tutor who tooted the flute
Tried to tutor two tooters to toot.
Said the two to the tutor:
Is it harder to toot, or
To tutor two tooters to toot?

☐ Verbs*

Verbs are 'doing' words. They are the words that show something happening or being. Verbs bring nouns to life.

Take an apple pie. It *is* not very interesting unless you *can do* something with it. But, as a very old English rhyme *tells* us, all sorts of things *can happen* to it if we *put* some verbs before it.

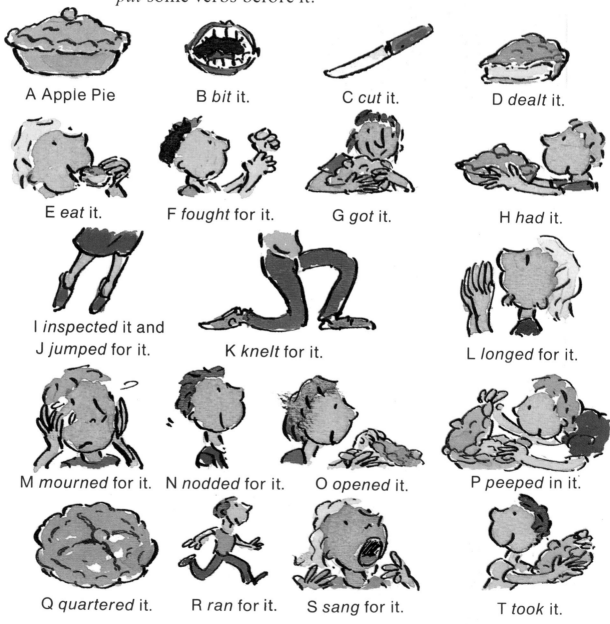

A Apple Pie   B *bit* it.   C *cut* it.   D *dealt* it.

E *eat* it.   F *fought* for it.   G *got* it.   H *had* it.

I *inspected* it and
J *jumped* for it.   K *knelt* for it.   L *longed* for it.

M *mourned* for it.   N *nodded* for it.   O *opened* it.   P *peeped* in it.

Q *quartered* it.   R *ran* for it.   S *sang* for it.   T *took* it.

UVWXYZ all *had* a slice and *went* off to bed.

28

Verbs are the key part of any sentence. A group of words *cannot make* a sentence unless it has at least one verb.

The black cat _____ the fish.

We could put many different words in this gap to make the whole part into a sentence: *licked, liked, pawed, sniffed, gobbled, spat at*, and *ate*.

Each verb can also change into many different tenses:
present – *eats* or *is eating*,
past – *was eating, ate, has eaten*, or *had eaten*.
future – *is going to eat, will eat*.
conditional – *would eat, would have eaten*.
And, of course, they can have negatives: *is not eating, did not eat, won't eat*, etc.

> The lion .... the mouse. You .... them.
> Can you *bring* these pairs of nouns and pronouns alive with verbs and other words?

As they say:

replied
murmured
shouted
interrupted

said

asked
jeered
cried
hissed
exclaimed

☐ **Wise words**

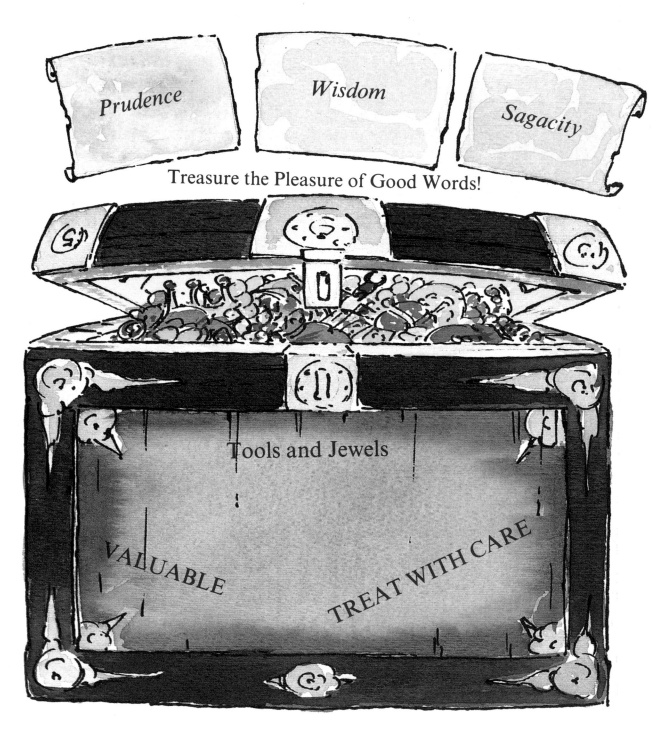

Prudence

Wisdom

Sagacity

Treasure the Pleasure of Good Words!

Tools and Jewels

VALUABLE

TREAT WITH CARE

Be wise!
Write, write and *write!*

Index